# YOU CAN DO
# AMAZING THINGS

YOU CAN DO AMAZING THINGS

An Hachette UK Company
www.hachette.co.uk

Vie Books, an imprint of Summersdale Publishers Ltd
Part of Octopus Publishing Group Limited
Carmelite House
50 Victoria Embankment
LONDON
EC4Y 0DZ
UK

www.summersdale.com

Printed and bound in the UK by Bell & Bain Ltd, Glasgow

ISBN: 978-1-80007-340-1

Substantial discounts on bulk quantities of Summersdale books are available to corporations, professional associations and other organizations. For details contact general enquiries: telephone: +44 (0) 1243 771107 or email: enquiries@summersdale.com.

# YOU CAN DO AMAZING THINGS

## A Child's Guide to Dealing with Change and New Challenges

Poppy O'Neill

# CONTENTS

# FOREWORD

*Amanda Ashman-Wymbs*
*Counsellor and Psychotherapist, registered and accredited by*
*the British Association for Counselling and Psychotherapy*

I have worked therapeutically with children in the public and private sector for many years and raised two daughters, and it is very clear to me that this insightful workbook is a much-needed tool in today's society. Supporting our children and young people to cope with change and enabling them to become more self-aware and develop greater resilience is part of a fundamental framework for their mental health and well-being, both now and throughout their lives.

Poppy O'Neill has provided many useful and effective therapeutic techniques and exercises in her book, drawing on cognitive and behavioural science, creative arts and mindfulness-based practices. It is written in a simple, warm and friendly way that will be clear, fun and attractive to the young reader. The child can use this book independently or with the support of their parent, teacher or carer. It encourages positive thinking, helps pave the way towards better emotional literacy and highlights the importance of kindness towards self and others. Through working with this book the child will become more aware of the resources they have within themselves and their lives. They will learn how to be more emotionally literate and how to think in more positive ways, as well as learning techniques to help them to feel calmer when things change and they are faced with challenges.

I highly recommend this book to support children to cope with changes, grow resilience and emotional intelligence and become more aware of, and modify, thought patterns that may be clouding their natural confidence.

# INTRODUCTION: A GUIDE FOR PARENTS AND CARERS

*You Can Do Amazing Things* is a practical guide to resilience for children. Using activities and ideas based on therapeutic techniques developed by child psychologists, this book will help your child to build their resilience, cope with change and view themselves in a more positive light.

Resilience is the ability to recover following difficulties. As your child grows, they'll encounter challenges, some of which can knock their confidence and be hard to bounce back from.

We all struggle with change sometimes – even when it's positive, it can be difficult in its own way – but your child might seem more sensitive and need more reassurance than others their age. Sometimes, no matter how much you support them through difficult times, they take longer than you'd expect to get used to new things. The truth is, resilience isn't about getting over emotional struggles – it's more to do with someone's ability to cope with whatever emotions they happen to experience.

This book is aimed at children aged 7–11, an age when lots of change occurs. School gets more serious, and there's the transition to the next stage of their education for many 10- and 11-year-olds. Friendships can become more complex, and the early stages of puberty mean changes in their bodies, too. Some children find having to deal with all these new experiences overwhelming. If this sounds like your child, you're not alone. With your support and understanding, it's possible for them to build up their resilience – bringing with it the confidence to navigate challenges, accept change and grow into a positive, dynamic young person.

## Signs of low resilience

Signs such as these are typical of children with low levels of resilience:

- Having trouble sleeping

- Finding it difficult to accept change or disagreements

- Dwelling on problems

- Keeping their emotions hidden

- Becoming very stressed when they make a mistake

If you recognize your child in this list, don't panic. It's important to remember that taking an interest in their emotional experiences can be a difficult step but it's also an incredibly positive one. It's OK if you're not sure what to do or how to help your child. Resilience is a lifelong habit rather than something that can be fixed or achieved quickly – meaning it's never too late to start building it.

# GETTING STARTED

Resilience is unique to each person, your child included, so it's hard to talk about it in specific terms. The best way to begin discussing emotions and emotional resilience is to simply ask about their day and see where the conversation goes. Try specific questions like these:

- What was funny today?
- What was annoying today?

If you sense that something is troubling them (the second question above can help with this!), gently ask more questions about that aspect of their day. In order to grow their resilience, your child needs to know that their feelings are accepted and understandable. So, when they talk about what makes them sad, angry or worried, it's really important to validate how they feel.

It can be tempting to minimize their concerns by explaining how problems can be solved, or why they needn't be worried. But while it may feel like the best and most sensible way to help them through difficult emotions, this approach can mean that children feel less comfortable talking about their feelings – making them harder to address. So, try to hold off solving the problem until later on.

Instead, listen to your child and show them that you understand. You could use phrases like "that sounds really scary/upsetting/difficult" to let them know that their feelings are welcome and make sense.

Resilience grows when we learn to trust that we will be OK, even if things don't go to plan. Let your child know that, whatever happens, you love them, and they can do difficult (and amazing) things.

## How to use this book: For parents and carers
. . . . . . . . . . . . . . . . . . . . . . . . . . . . . . . . . . . . . . . . . . . . . . . . . . . . . . . . . . . . . . . . . . . .

This book is for your child, so how involved you'll be will depend on them. Some children might be happy working through the pages by themselves, while others might want or need a little guidance and encouragement.

The activities are designed to get your child thinking about themselves and the way their mind works – let them know it's OK to ask for help and to set their own pace. Building resilience means trusting in their abilities and allowing them to make their own decisions.

Hopefully, this book will be helpful for you and your child, fostering greater understanding of how resilience works and how to build it. However, if you have any serious concerns about your child's mental health, your GP or health practitioner is the best person to go to for further advice.

# HOW TO USE THIS BOOK: A GUIDE FOR CHILDREN

How does it feel when things change? This could be a big thing, like moving house, or something like a last-minute delay to your bedtime routine. If change makes you feel worried, panicked or upset – you're not alone. It's very normal to find both big and small changes challenging.

Sometimes, though, worries about change can get in the way of being yourself and having fun. Here are some signs that this might be happening for you:

- You're scared to try new things in case something goes wrong

- You feel worried or angry about things for a long time after they happen

- Making a mistake feels really bad

- You hide your feelings from other people

If that sounds like you, you're not the only one! Lots of children feel this way – they just have different ways of showing it on the outside. This book is here to help you grow your resilience, get more comfortable with emotions and feel calm when changes happen.

There are lots of activities and ideas in this book to help you learn all about resilience, thoughts and emotions. You can go at your own pace, and you can ask your grown-up for help at any time – there might be things that you'd like to chat about with them, too. This book is for you and the activities are about you – so you're the expert!

# INTRODUCING ZIG THE MONSTER

Hello, I'm Zig! It's great to meet you. I'm here to guide you through this book. There are so many fun activities and interesting ideas – I can't wait to get started. Are you ready? Then let's go!

# PART 1:
# RESILIENCE AND ME

In this chapter we'll learn all about you, and all about resilience. Getting to know yourself is the first step to finding out just how amazing you are!

# WHAT IS RESILIENCE?

Resilience is the ability to cope when changes or challenges happen; it means knowing that although things might feel difficult right now, you will be OK. Being resilient doesn't mean you never feel angry, sad, worried or confused – in fact, resilient people feel all of these things. Changes and challenges can be:

- A new teacher at school

- Moving house

- Making a mistake

- You or someone in your family being ill

- Facing a fear

- Trying new things

- A change to your routine

Resilience is something you can grow, and going through changes and challenges can actually increase your level of resilience. This is because thinking back to a difficult experience can remind you that even though it felt bad at the time, you started to feel OK again afterward.

When something challenging happens – and even positive changes, like holidays, can be challenging! – it's OK to struggle with it. What's important is how kind you are to yourself while you're having a hard time: being kind to yourself is what true resilience is all about.

# ACTIVITY: ALL ABOUT ME

Let's find out all about you!

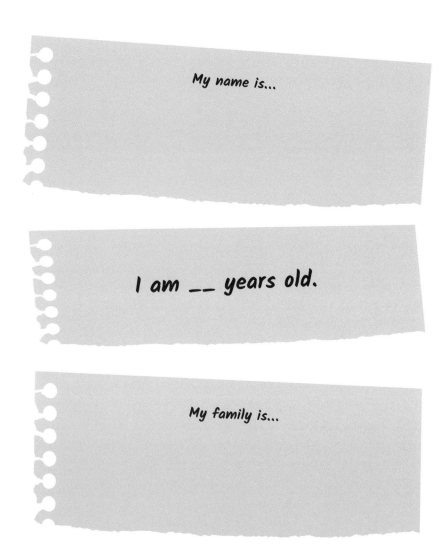

My name is...

I am __ years old.

My family is...

I'm amazing because...

I love to eat...

My favourite colour is...

# ACTIVITY: MY NAME POEM

Can you write a poem about you, using the letters of your name? Zig has written one:

**Z ingy**

**I maginative**

**G iggly**

This kind of poem is called an "acrostic". Now it's your turn! Think of a word that describes you for each of the letters of your name, and write your acrostic poem here:

*Write the letters of your name down the page here*

# SIGNS OF RESILIENCE

Everyone has resilience, but it can sometimes be hard to spot. Here are some signs of resilience:

- You try your best

- You talk about your feelings

- You speak up for yourself

- You don't give up if you make a mistake

- You take your time

- You're kind to yourself and others

# I AM ALWAYS DOING MY BEST

# COPING WITH CHANGE QUIZ

There are lots of different kinds of change that we have to deal with in life. This quiz will help you to see which ones are challenging for you.

**Your parents announce that you're going to another country on holiday in the summer. How do you feel?**
Anxious – so many things could go wrong
Excited – I love going to new places
Angry – why didn't they check with me first?

**You're at a friend's house and dinner is a new food you've never tried before. How do you feel?**
Panic – I find it really hard to try new foods and I don't want to
Relaxed – it looks tasty!
Awkward – I'll try a little bit just to be polite

> **You skipped your bath yesterday to watch a movie with your family, so now Dad says you need to have a bath, but it's not your normal night for it. How do you feel?**
>
> Annoyed – why can't he stick to the rules?
>
> Calm – I knew I'd need a bath, so a different day isn't a big deal
>
> Frustrated – the movie was silly and it isn't bath night

> **You've been excited for a trip to the beach all week, but when the day comes, it's raining heavily and you can't go. How do you feel?**
>
> Sad – I was really looking forward to that trip
>
> OK – I like staying at home better anyway
>
> Upset – why can't we wear raincoats and go anyway?

Whichever options you picked, your feelings and answers are OK and normal! There's no one way in which resilient people respond to change – resilience means being kind to yourself, whatever happens and however you're feeling.

# WHAT CHALLENGES DO KIDS YOUR AGE DEAL WITH?

Everyone faces challenges, and you can't tell from looking at someone what they're struggling with. Here are some of the things that children your age find hard to deal with:

- Friendships

- Going on holiday/vacation

- Moving house

- Starting a new school

- Going to the doctor or dentist

- Being told "no"

- Having to wait

- Relationships with brothers and sisters

Some of these might sound difficult to you, and others might seem like no big deal. The challenges you have might not be on the list. Emotions are complicated and everyone is different!

Big changes like these are very difficult to deal with. You don't need to cope with these things on your own.

# WHAT'S CHALLENGING FOR ME?

Different people find different things easy or hard. To do hard things, you need resilience. What takes resilience for you?

Colour the things that you find really difficult in red, the things that are a bit tricky in yellow and use green for the ones that are easy for you. Add some of your own if you think of them!

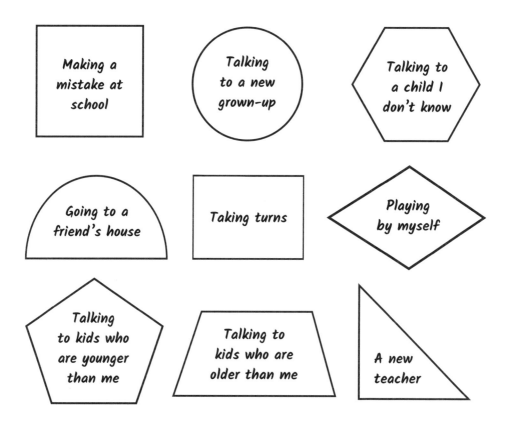

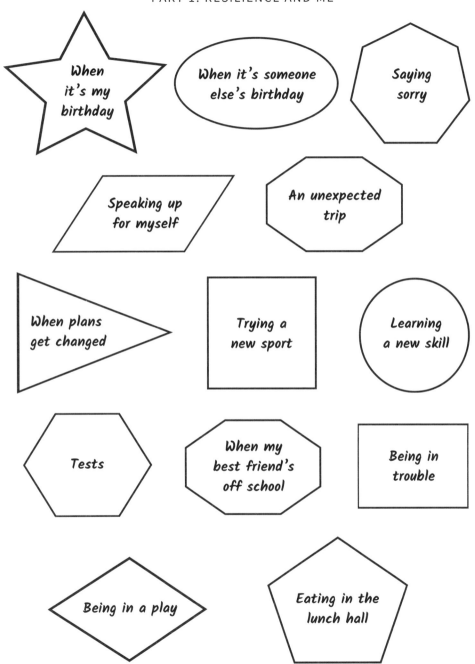

When it's my birthday

When it's someone else's birthday

Saying sorry

Speaking up for myself

An unexpected trip

When plans get changed

Trying a new sport

Learning a new skill

Tests

When my best friend's off school

Being in trouble

Being in a play

Eating in the lunch hall

# ACTIVITY: A TIME I WAS RESILIENT

Can you think of a time when you were resilient? Perhaps you did something challenging – like saying sorry after you'd upset a friend – or were kind to yourself while feeling difficult emotions.

_____

_____

Can you remember anything that helped you to feel extra brave and resilient?

_____

_____

How could you use your answer to the last question to help you find resilience today and in the future?

_____

_____

- **Remembering times when you were resilient is a great way of building up your resilience for the future.**

# PART 2: RESILIENCE BOOSTERS AND SHRINKERS

Some days you feel like a superhero – strong, resilient and ready to take on the world! But other days can be more difficult. Learning about when and why we feel the way we feel will help you to find resilience whenever you need it. In this chapter we'll take a look at all the things that can shrink your resilience, as well as lots of ways to boost it.

# ACTIVITY: TAKE A DEEP BREATH

We breathe all day long, without even thinking about it. But did you know that concentrating on taking deep breaths is an amazing way to boost your confidence, bravery and resilience?

You can even use your own hand to supercharge your breathing. Starting at the base of your thumb, slowly trace your finger up and down over your whole hand. On the way up, breathe in; on the way down, breathe out.

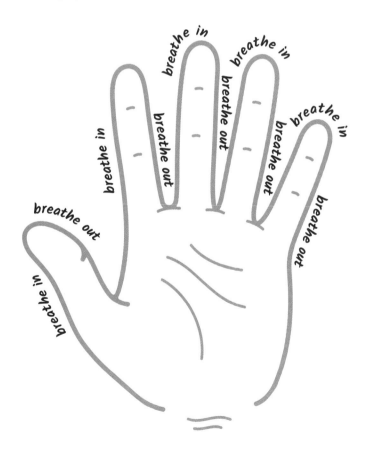

Use this page to draw around your own hand! Can you add "breathe out" and "breathe in" instructions?

Focusing on your breathing for five breaths is enough to calm your mind and body, making you feel more resilient.

# ACTIVITY: WHAT SHRINKS YOUR RESILIENCE?

What are the things that shrink your resilience? Perhaps they make you feel shy, scared or upset, or they make you want to curl up into a ball, run away or disappear in a puff of smoke.

Resilience shrinkers might be a type of place – like somewhere that's loud or busy. They can be thoughts – such as the idea that people will laugh at you – or things other people say to you, like when someone tells you not to feel the way you feel. Or it can be a situation like when plans change or someone disagrees with you.

Write a list of things that shrink your resilience here:

_____

_____

_____

_____

_____

It's OK if you don't feel resilient all the time – no one does! In the next chapter we'll learn about how to be resilient, even when one of these things is happening.

# QUICK RESILIENCE BOOSTERS

When you need to feel good about yourself in a hurry, try one of these tried-and-tested resilience boosters.

- ☼ Talk about how you feel
- ☼ Get up and move around
- ☼ Cuddle a pet
- ☼ Take a break from what you're doing

- ☼ Do something creative
- ☼ Take a deep breath
- ☼ Sing
- ☼ Drum your hands on your knees

These tips help emotions to feel more comfortable and less serious, because they encourage you to pay attention to your body rather than your thoughts.

# ACTIVITY: MINDFUL COLOURING

Mindfulness is about paying attention to what's happening at this moment, and it's a brilliant way of boosting resilience! When you stop thinking about what's already happened, and stop worrying about what might happen in the future, you can fully enjoy what you're doing right now.

Colouring is an amazing mindful activity. Watch how your pens or pencils fill the page with colour, listen to the sound they make on the paper and notice how they feel in your hand.

- **Try not to worry about making a perfect picture – just enjoy it!**

# ACTIVITY: WHAT IF THE BEST HAPPENS?

When we're facing changes and challenges, we often imagine that things will turn out really badly. Zig is going on an aeroplane for the first time and is imagining what it might be like.

It's OK to think these things – they might come true. And if they do, Zig will be OK. But here's an idea… What if things turn out brilliantly? What if…

Can you think of something you're worried about in the future? First, write or draw your worries here:

Now, try to imagine it going as well as it could possibly go. What would that be like? Write or draw your ideas here:

Imagining a good outcome boosts resilience by allowing some positive thoughts into your mind, even if you still feel worried.

I AM
STRONG

# ACTIVITY: POSITIVE AFFIRMATIONS

Affirmations are short sentences that help you to be kind to yourself, and remind you just how brilliant and resilient you are. They're a really simple and useful way to deal with changes and challenges – all you need to do is say one to yourself.

Different affirmations feel good to different people. Read these resilience-boosting affirmations, and pick a handful that make you feel calm and strong:

Write your chosen affirmation, or affirmations, here:

# ACTIVITY: HELP ZIG FEEL BRAVE

One morning at school, Zig had a tummy ache.

After lunch, Zig's tummy ache got worse.

At reading time, Zig was sick. Everybody in Zig's class saw and Zig had to go home to rest for a couple of days. Zig feels embarrassed about being sick in front of the class.

Now Zig is feeling well again, it's time to go back to school. How do you think Zig is feeling about returning to school?

What might help Zig to feel brave when it's time for school?

If you were in Zig's class, what's something you could say to Zig?

Doing difficult things that take bravery – like returning to school after feeling embarrassed – builds resilience. But when we do hard things and the people around us are kind and welcoming, it supercharges our resilience!

# ACTIVITY: MAKE A PAINTED PEBBLE

Being creative helps you to deal with change and challenges, because it encourages your mind to make sense of the world in a relaxed, playful way. All kinds of creativity are good for boosting resilience: writing stories, making up games, dancing, singing, painting, colouring… anything you can think of!

Here's a fun creative activity you can do at home.

## You will need:

-  Acrylic paints

-  A paintbrush

- Pebbles

## How to:

1. Use the paintbrush to draw pictures or patterns on the pebbles – if they have interesting bumps or textures, use these to inspire your painting!
2. Let the paint dry and keep your painted pebble for yourself, give it to someone you know as a gift or leave it outdoors for a stranger to find.

MY FEELINGS
MATTER

# EVERYONE IS DIFFERENT

Every single human being has different strengths and challenges. Sometimes it can feel lonely, especially if it seems like you're the only one struggling with a change that's happening. It's important to realize that not everybody shows their feelings on the outside. In fact, it takes a huge amount of bravery to show that you are having a hard time – that's why lots of people keep their feelings inside, or only show them to their parents or carers.

Messages about how you "should" feel about different challenges and changes come to you every day – from TV, books, people around you, adverts and the internet. Often, children are told not to worry or to "look on the bright side" when changes happen – but that's not very helpful.

How you feel is how you feel, and it's OK to say so. Not everyone will feel the same way, and that's fine – no one is right or wrong when it comes to feelings. Real resilience means being yourself and getting comfy with other people being themselves, too.

# ACTIVITY: TALKING ABOUT FEELINGS

Sometimes it feels difficult to talk about how you're feeling, but it really does help. Talking lets worries out of your mind and, when the other person is a good listener, it makes you feel better and your worries feel smaller.

Who do you know that you feel comfortable talking to? You can pick as many people as you like. What are your favourite things about them?

# A GROWTH MINDSET

Having a growth mindset means believing that you can always learn more, whatever happens.

Imagine a plant that's just grown its first leaf.

The plant could think: "I'm shorter than the others, and I hate the rain!"

Or it could think:

*I'm growing bigger every day, and the rain helps me!*

You are like the plant, and the raindrops are like challenges. These feel difficult or uncomfortable, but each one helps you to learn new things and grow a little more. When you have a growth mindset, you know that mistakes, changes and bad days are all part of how we learn.

Even a big plant like this one is still growing new leaves. Can you colour it in?

# WHAT BOOSTS YOUR RESILIENCE?

Now we've learned lots of different ways to boost resilience, it's time to think about you. What makes you feel confident, patient and calm? It could be an activity from this book, a person you know or something else.

Can you think of something new you'd like to try, next time you need a boost?

# I AM ALWAYS LEARNING AND CHANGING

# PART 3: BUILDING RESILIENCE

Resilience is something you can grow, like a tree, and you can do that by being kind to yourself and doing brave things. This will also help you to deal with life's changes and challenges. In this chapter we'll look at ways you can build up your resilience, helping you to feel calm and in control.

# WHERE DOES RESILIENCE COME FROM?

Resilience can come from remembering a time when you were scared but things turned out OK, and it can come from knowing that you're brave, even when things are scary.

Imagine the first time you saw a thunderstorm – it must have been very frightening, because it was loud and strange, and you weren't sure what would happen. Perhaps you thought the sky was falling down! Now you're older, you've probably seen plenty of thunderstorms, and you know that, although they can still feel scary while they're happening, you'll be OK. That's the kind of resilience that comes from memories.

Resilience also comes from being kind to yourself and expressing your feelings – check out Parts 5 and 6 for ideas on how to do this. When something scary or upsetting happens – like starting a new school and saying goodbye to your friends – it's very natural to feel a lot of emotions. You might feel sad, angry, worried and excited, all at the same time. Resilience is when you have room in your heart for all your feelings, and you know that none of them will last forever. So, the kinder you are to your heart, the more resilient you'll be.

# COPING WITH SETBACKS

Sometimes things don't go the way we plan them. Perhaps you don't get the birthday gift you were hoping for, or your cousin wins the board game instead of you. It feels really disappointing when these things happen, and disappointment is a difficult emotion to deal with – it takes resilience to bounce back from setbacks.

When you feel disappointed, just like any other big emotion, you can use one of your resilience boosters. Talk about your feelings, move your body, do a breathing exercise or ask your grown-up for a hug. You don't need to hide your feelings, but resilience means welcoming them and letting them out in a way that's cool, calm and in control.

# FEELINGS HILL

When a big feeling starts to build up inside you, it can feel really scary. Big emotions usually happen in the shape of a hill, like this:

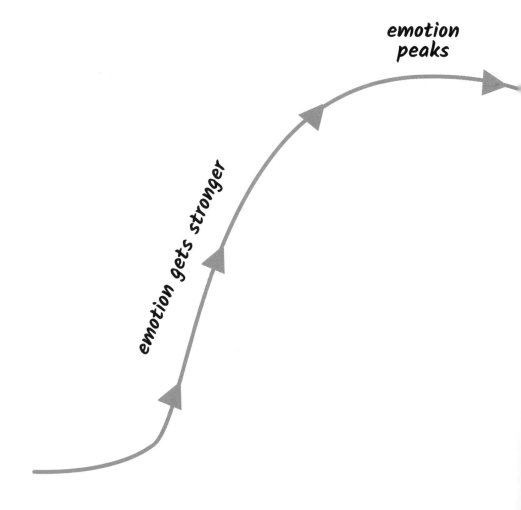

When you feel a big emotion, like anxiety, imagine this picture. The top of the hill is where you feel really anxious – perhaps your heart is beating faster, and you feel quite panicky. When you feel like this, remember that the emotion is about to get easier and calmer. Just keep breathing until you feel in control again.

Every time you do this, you're being really brave and building your resilience.

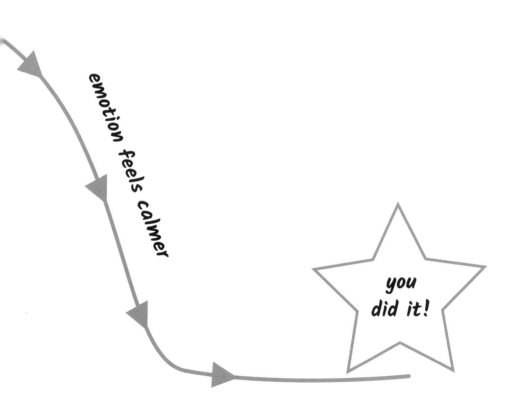

emotion feels calmer

you did it!

# MAGICAL MISTAKES

Mistakes are one of the main ingredients of resilience. Building resilience helps you to keep trying after getting something wrong, and making mistakes helps to build resilience! You might think that making zero mistakes is a good thing, but you'd be wrong.

Getting things 100 per cent perfectly right first time is not how human beings learn.

Think about something you have mastered and can now do right first time, without even thinking about it… something like walking, talking or eating food. These are all skills that you had to learn when you were small. Everyone – even you, even your teacher – dribbled baby food down their chin, before learning how to get it into their tummy.

It's the same with maths problems, riding a bike, learning the words to a song – anything you want to learn, you have to get it wrong at least a few times before you master it.

Mistakes are so magical because we remember them better than the parts we get right. Because making mistakes makes us feel emotions like embarrassment or anger, our brains remember them much more vividly, and we're less likely to repeat them. So making a mistake and feeling an emotion about it doesn't mean you're doing something wrong – it's your brain's way of helping you to learn faster.

# THOUGHTS AREN'T FACTS

Our thoughts are one of the things that make it difficult to be kind to our feelings and grow resilience. Our brains love to make up stories and try to predict the future, but the truth is that thoughts are not facts.

Unhelpful thoughts will shrink your resilience, and make you feel bad about yourself and scared of the world around you.

One way to deal with unhelpful thoughts is to question them – like a detective. This will help you to work out if the thought is worth keeping in your head or not.

- Am I being fair to myself?

- Is it helpful for me to think this?

- Is it likely to be true?

- Is it based on facts?

- Can I think of a fact that proves it wrong?

- Is it a kind thing to say?

Zig is having a thought and it's making Zig feel awful! Can you help Zig question this thought?

Other unhelpful thoughts might include:

No one
likes me

Bad things always
happen to me

I'll feel
sad forever

I always get
things wrong

If things aren't
perfect, I'm bad

I LIKE MYSELF

# ACTIVITY: TRANSFORM YOUR THOUGHTS

If you're stuck with an unhelpful, resilience-shrinking thought, there's always a resilience-boosting way of looking at it – you just need to find it! Changing the way you think might feel strange at first, but the more you practise, the easier it will be. Thinking positively is a wonderful way to build resilience.

The secret to turning unhelpful thoughts into positive ones is kindness! Here's how it's done…

Unhelpful thought:

Add some kindness:

When you transform the thought into one that's kinder, you can believe in yourself, do your best and keep going. Kindness helps you to grow resilience.

Now it's your turn – can you think of an unhelpful thought? Maybe it's one you've had, or one that's on your mind sometimes. Write it here:

Can you transform it into a kinder thought?

Now, when the unhelpful thought pops into your head, you can think (or say out loud!) your kinder thought instead.

# ACTIVITY: I CAN DO HARD THINGS!

When you feel sure that you can handle changes and challenges, your resilience grows. Can you think of a time you found something hard to deal with? Perhaps a trip you were looking forward to was cancelled, or a new baby was born in your family. Write about it here:

How do you feel when you think about this situation? Circle any that sound right to you:

**Angry**          **Scared**          **Anxious**          **Like running away**

**Like hiding**          **Embarrassed**          **Tired**          **Frozen to the spot**

If none of those are quite right, you can write your own:

How does it feel in your body? You can use words, patterns, colours and symbols – whichever work best for you – to show your feelings on the diagram:

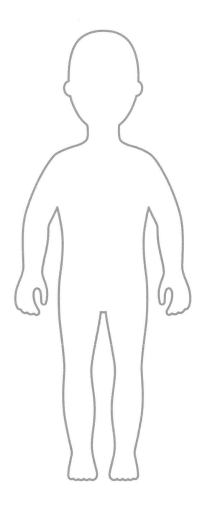

Building your resilience is hard work and you're doing amazingly well. On the next few pages you'll find useful tools that will help you to handle tricky situations.

# ALL FEELINGS ARE OK

Everyone has emotions, but most people don't always show them on the outside, so if you're feeling a difficult or big emotion, it can seem like you're the only one.

When you remember that all emotions are OK, and that none of them can harm you or stop you from doing hard things, you unlock the secret to resilience in any situation.

If you feel scared, that's OK – you can ask for help and reassurance, feel your fear, and you can be brave at the same time.

If you feel sad, that's OK – you can cry, ask for a hug and feel your sadness, and you can be brave at the same time.

If you feel angry, that's OK – you can move your body, talk about your feelings and feel your anger, and you can be brave at the same time.

# ACTIVITY: BE MINDFUL

Mindfulness means awareness. When we practice being mindful, we focus all our attention on the present. When things are tricky and you're having a hard time, you can use mindfulness to help your mind and body to feel calm.

Here's how:

- Stop what you're doing

- Put one hand on your heart and the other on your belly

- Take a deep breath in and feel your belly grow bigger

- Say to yourself – silently or out loud – "I am feeling _____"

- Take another deep breath

- Say to yourself – silently or out loud – "I am safe. It's OK to feel _____"

# ACTIVITY: TAKE YOUR TIME

Slowing down and doing things at your own pace is one of the keys to building resilience. When you don't hurry yourself to do things that feel uncomfortable to you before you're ready, you learn to trust yourself and feel confident.

Zig is starting a new school, but isn't ready to join any after-school clubs yet. That's OK! Zig wants to settle in first, then give a club a try. Knowing that this is OK helps Zig to relax and feel comfortable at the new school. Even if the other students do after-school clubs, it's OK for Zig to make a different choice.

Have a think about a change or challenge that's coming up in the future for you. What parts of it feel OK and comfortable? What parts would you like to take your time with? What are you not OK with?

What feels OK now:

_____

_____

_____

_____

What I'd like to take my time with:

_____

_____

_____

_____

What I'm not OK with right now:

_____

_____

_____

I CAN GO AT
MY OWN PACE

# ACTIVITY: SLOW DOWN WITH SENSES

Taking your time can seem tricky when you're feeling big emotions, like anger and fear, because they can make us feel panicky and like we need to take action right away.

Tuning into the senses can help you to slow down, and calm your body and mind.

Here's how:

Spot one thing that you can sense with each of your five senses:

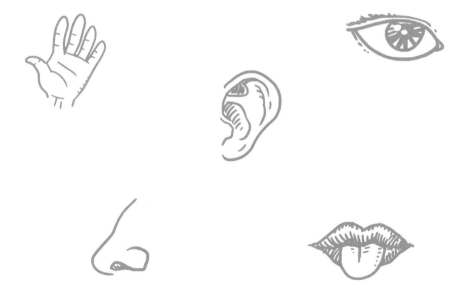

You can keep thinking of sets of five things until you feel calm.

Try it now! Write or draw below…

One thing I can see:

One thing I can hear:

One thing I can touch:

One thing I can smell:

One thing I can taste:

# SPEAKING UP

Just because your resilience is growing, and you can do difficult and amazing things, it doesn't mean that you shouldn't speak up when you're struggling. Remember – resilience is about being kind to yourself, and that means taking good care of you!

Worrying about how other people will react when you speak up for yourself is a big resilience shrinker. In reality, you can't control other people's emotions or actions. As long as you are telling the truth when you speak up, you're doing the right thing.

# ACTIVITY: WHAT I CAN AND CAN'T CONTROL

Wouldn't it be amazing if you could control the weather, or time, or the rules at school? You could have lots of fun with a magic power like that. But it might also be quite hard work being in charge of big, important things. In real life, you're in control of:

## *Your actions*

## *Your words*

And that's pretty good news for your resilience. It can be easy to feel worried, angry or scared about things you can't control, especially if you're going through a difficult time or a big change. But remembering that the only things you have control over are your words and actions can make you feel stronger and calmer, because it means you can give your brain a break from thinking about all the other things.

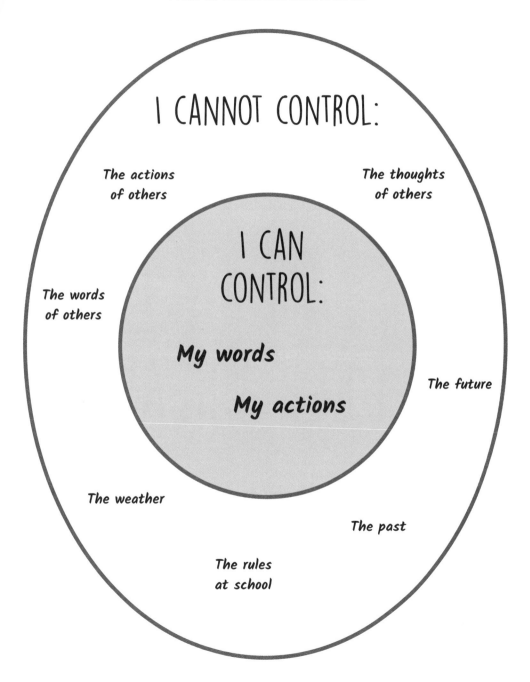

# PART 4:
## DEALING WITH CHANGE

Change is when we need resilience most. When there's something new to get used to in your life, all sorts of feelings might come up, and it can be a confusing time. In this chapter we'll find out why changes are so difficult, and how to deal with them.

# WHY IS CHANGE DIFFICULT?

Our brains love to know exactly what's going to happen, and any small change of activity means they aren't 100 per cent sure what'll happen next – there are gaps in the information, and gaps in information are a brain's least favourite thing. Big and small changes can feel really difficult to accept because they set an alarm off in our brains.

An example of a small change could be getting out of bed in the morning. In your bed it's cosy and warm, and you've just had a lovely sleep. Now your alarm clock is telling you it's time to get up and ready for school. Your brain says: "No, thank you. If I get up, I won't be cosy anymore. I'll have to do boring things like brushing teeth, and I'm not sure if today will go well or not. I want to stay in bed, where it's warm and familiar."

Another example is to go from playing one game to another. Even if both games are fun, it takes energy for your brain and body to switch to a new activity.

Bigger changes – like starting a new school – work in the same way. But because they have a bigger effect on your life, they feel more difficult. Your brain has all sorts of gaps in its information – who will you sit next to? What time is lunch? Will Dad know where to meet you at the end of the day?

I CAN CHALLENGE MYSELF

# WHAT KINDS OF CHANGE ARE TRICKY?

You can do amazing things! Kids your age face all sorts of changes in their lives with bravery and resilience – here are just some of the things people deal with:

- Cancelled plans

- New school

- New brothers and sisters

- Divorce

- Loss of loved ones

- News stories that affect everyday life

- Rule changes

- Changes to routine

You might have had to deal with some of the changes on this list, or perhaps there's something you find hard that isn't mentioned. If you'd like to add your own, you can write it here:

_____

_____

_____

# ZIG'S NEW HOUSE

Zig is moving house, and everything is changing! It means Zig's family will live further away from school, so they will need to drive there each morning. There's a new street to get used to, a new bedroom, a new cupboard to fit toys in, a new bathtub…

Zig liked things the way they were before and is finding it hard to feel OK with all the changes.

Zig's carers can see how hard this is. Here are some of the things they do to help Zig feel OK:

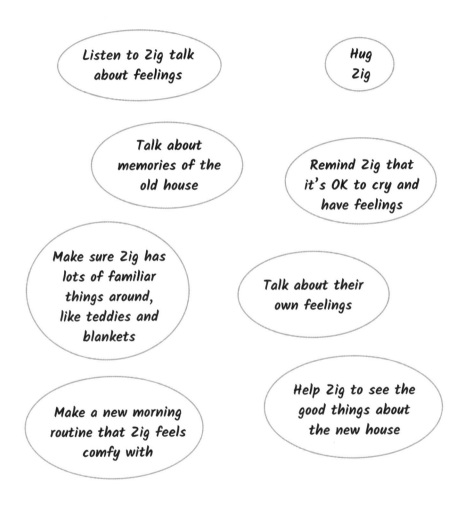

Listen to Zig talk about feelings

Hug Zig

Talk about memories of the old house

Remind Zig that it's OK to cry and have feelings

Make sure Zig has lots of familiar things around, like teddies and blankets

Talk about their own feelings

Make a new morning routine that Zig feels comfy with

Help Zig to see the good things about the new house

The people who love and care for us are really important, especially when we're going through a change. You can show your grown-up this page if you'd like help with feeling OK when things are changing.

# ACTIVITY: A TIME SOMETHING CHANGED

Can you think of a time when something in your life changed? Perhaps it's one of those listed on page 79, or something else.

Write or draw about it here:

How did you feel about the change?

Who or what helped you to feel OK?

You're brave and resilient, and you can do amazing things!

CHANGE
IS A PART
OF LIFE

# ACTIVITY: WHO CAN I TALK TO?

Your good friends and the grown-ups who care for you want to hear what it's like to be you, so don't be afraid to talk to people you trust, if you're struggling with a change that's happening in your life.

Even if you're worried your feelings don't quite make sense, or if you're not sure how your emotions will make the other person feel, it's still OK to talk about them.

Talking about your feelings, worries and challenges is one of the simplest and best ways to feel better and build resilience. When things – big or small – change, it's normal to have all sorts of feelings, and sharing them is a sign of resilience.

Who are the people in your life that you feel comfortable talking to about anything and everything? Draw them here – just one person is enough; two or three is plenty, and if you have more, that's great!

# ACTIVITY: MAKE A COMIC STRIP

If there's a change of plan, or you're going somewhere you haven't been before, it can feel really uncomfortable. Your brain comes up with all sorts of questions about what might happen, which can make you feel very worried.

Ask a grown-up to help you make a comic strip so you can get a good idea of what will or could happen, which tells your brain that there's a plan and it's OK to relax.

Zig's going on an aeroplane for the very first time! Zig's grown-ups make a comic strip with Zig.

First, Zig comes up with some big questions:

They make a comic strip together, like this:

1: At 7 a.m., we'll get in the car and leave for the airport

2: At the airport, we'll check in our bags and show our passports

3: If I feel uncomfortable on the plane, I can hold Mum's hand, listen to an audiobook or talk about my feelings

4: The plane will land and we'll get a taxi to our hotel

You can use this page to make your own comic strip! You can draw about any kind of change, new challenge or thing that you feel unsure about.

|  |  |
|--|--|
|  |  |
|  |  |

# ACTIVITY: LOOKING FOR RAINBOWS

If you don't look up on a rainy day, you'll never see a rainbow. The same is true for positives – the more you look for good things, the more you'll find.

Resilient people look for reasons to feel calm and happy, even when they're dealing with a tricky situation. This doesn't mean you can't feel negative emotions, or that you need to ignore negative things – resilience is all about finding a balance between the two.

Zig was looking forward to Bop's birthday party this weekend, but it's been cancelled because of the snow. Zig feels down – it's really disappointing when plans are cancelled.

Zig cries and talks about how it feels.

Then, when the disappointed feeling starts to move out of Zig's body, Zig is ready to start thinking about positives. Bop's party will happen another day… Today Zig can go and play in the snow!

Can you help Zig find the rainbow in this maze?

# FEEL CURIOUS

Some changes are hard to feel positive about, and you don't need to force yourself, if it's too difficult. Instead, you can try looking for things to feel curious about.

If you're ill, you could feel curious about what's happening in your body, or how any medicine you take works.

If there's going to be a new baby in the family, you could feel curious about what they'll look like, or what kind of person they'll grow into.

If your best friend has moved away, you can feel curious about their new home, and send them a letter with lots and lots of questions.

Feeling curious leads the imagination toward new ideas and makes it a lot easier to feel OK when things are changing.

# ACTIVITY: KEEP A JOURNAL

Try keeping a journal when something is changing in your life. Writing down your feelings and thoughts will build your resilience a little more, every time you do it. This is because writing helps to take worried thoughts out of your mind, making you feel calmer and more in control.

Every day, write about the things that happened and how you felt, and then find one challenge and one thing you were thankful for.

**Monday**

_____

_____

Today was challenging when _____

I was thankful for_____

**Tuesday**

_____

_____

Today was challenging when _____

I was thankful for_____

## Wednesday

_____

_____

Today was challenging when _____

I was thankful for_____

## Thursday

_____

_____

Today was challenging when _____

I was thankful for_____

## Friday

_____

_____

Today was challenging when _____

I was thankful for_____

**Saturday**

_____

_____

Today was challenging when _____

I was thankful for_____

**Sunday**

_____

_____

Today was challenging when _____

I was thankful for_____

Taking time every day to think about your feelings and experiences will help you to build resilience, be kind to yourself and get in the habit of looking for positives.

# ACTIVITY: ASKING FOR HELP

As we know, resilience doesn't mean squashing down your feelings or pretending not to have them. Sometimes, we all need help to deal with change – but asking for help can feel really tricky.

If there's something that would make the change feel easier for you, it's OK to ask a grown-up. It might not always be possible to do things exactly as you'd like them, but it will give that grown-up a better idea of what's tricky for you and help them to come up with ideas.

Lucy's class is starting swimming lessons, but she finds swimming hats really uncomfortable to wear – they feel hot, itchy and tight on her head. Her teacher doesn't know this, so Lucy asks her if she can swim without one.

Now Lucy's teacher knows what's difficult for her, she can do her best to help. She telephones the swimming instructor, who says it would be OK, as long as Lucy puts her hair up.

Lucy feels OK with putting her hair up, and the swimming instructor feels OK that everyone is safe in the pool.

I CAN ASK
FOR HELP

# PART 5: TAKING GOOD CARE OF YOU

Taking care of your body will help you to feel your best and deal with whatever the day brings. In this chapter we'll learn all about why being kind to your body and mind makes you calm, strong and resilient.

# WHY DOES TAKING CARE OF YOURSELF MAKE YOU MORE RESILIENT?

Emotions happen in the body and mind, so the healthier and better they feel, the easier it is to deal with whichever emotions come up.

Think about it: when you're hungry, thirsty or tired, are you at your best? Probably not – most of us get grumpy and impatient… Zig certainly does!

How about when you're worried about something and it's filling up all your thoughts… Add a change to your plans or a tricky situation and it can quickly feel overwhelming.

Since we can't always plan ahead for changes and challenges, taking care of our bodies and minds is something we need to do every day. Feeling good builds resilience, so let's feel good!

# ACTIVITY: MY BEDTIME ROUTINE

Doing the same things in the same order every evening will help your mind and body to feel relaxed and ready for bed. This will help you to get a good night's sleep and feel full of energy in the morning.

What's in your bedtime routine? Circle the words below and add your own, if Zig's missed any!

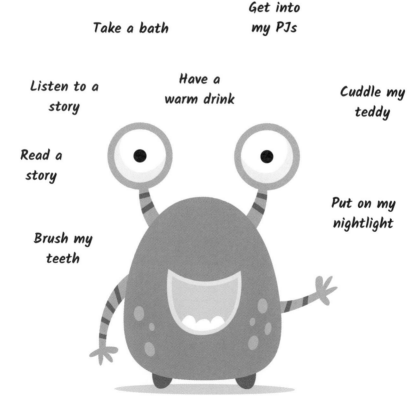

Take a bath

Get into my PJs

Listen to a story

Have a warm drink

Cuddle my teddy

Read a story

Put on my nightlight

Brush my teeth

Draw or write each step in your bedtime routine, in order, in the boxes:

# DRINKING PLENTY OF WATER

Not having enough water in our bodies can have a big effect! We might feel tired, anxious and grumpy; our heads might ache and our hearts beat faster. That's why it's important to drink plenty of water – about six cups a day is best.

Water is amazing! Did you know…

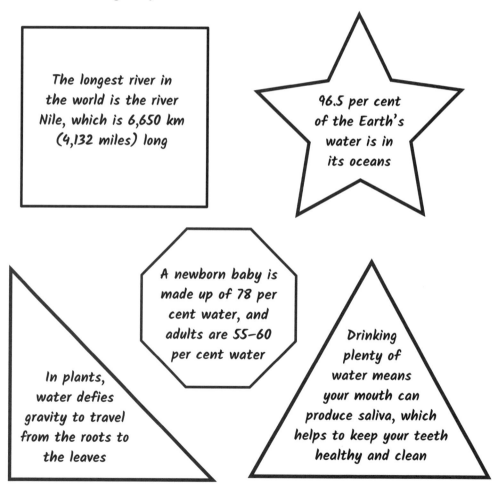

The longest river in the world is the river Nile, which is 6,650 km (4,132 miles) long

96.5 per cent of the Earth's water is in its oceans

A newborn baby is made up of 78 per cent water, and adults are 55–60 per cent water

In plants, water defies gravity to travel from the roots to the leaves

Drinking plenty of water means your mouth can produce saliva, which helps to keep your teeth healthy and clean

# GLORIOUS FOOD

Eating a good range of food is a big part of building resilience. When you feed your body what it needs, you feel better able to cope with changes and challenges.

Listen to your body – it is very wise, and will tell you when it's hungry and when it's had enough to eat!

What's your favourite food?

# ACTIVITY: YUMMY SPINACH PESTO

Spinach is packed with all the nutrients that boost resilience: iron, vitamins A, C and K, B vitamins, and protein. Spinach tastes great on its own or in lots of different dishes – why not make spinach pesto to share with your family?

*You will need:*

- Handful of fresh basil leaves
- Handful of fresh spinach leaves
- 1/3 cup ground almonds (or other ground nuts or seeds)
- 25 g (1 oz) grated Cheddar cheese
- 1 small clove of garlic – sliced
- Olive oil to taste
- Food blender – or sharp knife and chopping board

*How to:*

1. Ask an adult to help you put all the dry ingredients in your blender, or on a chopping board if you're chopping by hand.
2. Blend or chop into very small pieces, until the juice from the leaves has made everything slightly sticky and all the ingredients are mixed together.
3. Transfer the mixture into a bowl and slowly pour in the olive oil, until the pesto becomes a soft paste (you can always add more later if you want it to be runnier).

Try eating this delicious pesto with pasta, as a dip or spread on toast!

# TIME TO CHILL OUT

How do you like to relax? Finding time to unwind every day will help you to build resilience and feel good about yourself.

Here are some relaxing activities that you can try.

- Learn a dance. Learning any new skill builds resilience, because you have to keep practising to get it right. Dancing is a fun and relaxing idea for learning something new.

- Play a card game. With others or by yourself, playing card games takes patience, which is a brilliant resilience builder.

- Read a book. Learning about a character or an idea will expand your mind, making you kinder, wiser and better able to deal with challenges.

- Try a drawing tutorial. Learn how to draw something new – you'll be surprised what you can do when you break a task down into steps.

- Do a puzzle. Try sudoku, a crossword or a maths problem to really get your brain working. Puzzles help you to learn new ways of thinking, making you more flexible and able to cope with change.

I CAN
GO WITH
THE FLOW

# ACTIVITY: HOW ARE YOU DOING?

Building your resilience and coping with life's changes is hard work! It's important to take some time to check in with yourself and see how you're feeling each day.

Ask yourself:

Is my breathing fast or slow?

Do I feel any aches?

What emotions am I feeling?

Am I thirsty, hungry or tired?

Do I want to move my body or be still?

What's tricky for me right now?

What's going well for me right now?

Use the space below to write or draw about how you're feeling.

# EVERY DAY IS A NEW ADVENTURE

# ACTIVITY: DO SOME YOGA STRETCHES

Stretching your body makes you feel instantly calmer and more confident – it's a brilliant way to help yourself feel more relaxed when you're facing something challenging.

Try these yoga stretches when you need a boost.

If you haven't tried these yoga poses before, please ask your grown-up to refer to a yoga book or online resource.

Cow pose

Cat pose

Warrior pose

Tree pose

Downward-facing dog

Forward fold

Cobra pose

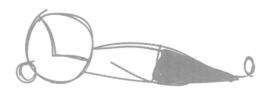

Corpse pose

# ACTIVITY: MAKE A TINY HOUSE

A natural environment – whether that's the woods, the beach or your own garden – is a great place to build strong resilience and skills to deal with change. When you're out in nature, there are so many opportunities for creativity, problem-solving and curiosity.

Here's a fun activity to try next time you're outdoors!

**You will need:**

- String (optional)
- Clay (optional)
- Your imagination!

**How to:**

1. Find a spot to build your tiny house for an elf or fairy – anywhere that could act as walls or support for your building is great, such as among tree roots, leaning against a wall or next to a pile of stones.
2. Using whatever natural materials you find nearby – stones, sticks, leaves, shells – plus any clay or string you've brought with you, use your imagination to build your tiny house. You can make furniture and characters to go inside: be as creative as you like!

# PART 6:
## TIME TO CHILL

The more time you spend feeling relaxed and calm, the better you'll be able to cope with difficult situations and unexpected changes. That's because your mind grows strong and capable when you're relaxing and having fun. This chapter is all about chilling out, so read on for some fun and calming activities.

# ACTIVITY: GET CREATIVE

Your mind is at its most powerful when you're being creative in any way –
making art, writing stories, inventing games or any other activity that uses
your imagination. It's then that your brain builds new pathways and gets more
skilful at solving problems, coming up with ideas and managing emotions.

Use this space to invent a machine that will help people to relax. Don't be
afraid to use magic and to be silly – let your imagination guide you.

# ACTIVITY: TAKE A MINDFUL WALK

Mindfulness means paying attention to your senses and focusing on the present moment. Walking mindfully could involve looking all around you and noticing the interesting things you encounter.

Go for a mindful walk with your grown-up in your local neighbourhood and play spotting games – pick one of the following lists and tick each item off when you see it:

| | |
|---|---|
| ☐ | Something square |
| ☐ | Something circle-shaped |
| ☐ | Something triangle-shaped |
| ☐ | Something oval |
| ☐ | Something star-shaped |

| | |
|---|---|
| ☐ | Something red |
| ☐ | Something orange |
| ☐ | Something yellow |
| ☐ | Something green |
| ☐ | Something blue |
| ☐ | Something purple |
| ☐ | Something pink |
| ☐ | Something black |
| ☐ | Something brown |
| ☐ | Something white |

- [ ] Something you can see
- [ ] Something you can hear
- [ ] Something that has a smell
- [ ] Something that looks interesting to touch
- [ ] Something that has a taste

- [ ] Something liquid
- [ ] Something solid
- [ ] Something that's a gas
- [ ] Something natural
- [ ] Something made by humans

# ACTIVITY: CHILL-OUT ZONE

Your room is where you can go to relax and recharge your batteries. Having a calm, cosy space is a really important part of taking care of ourselves, which is a big part of building resilience.

Can you decorate this bedroom to be the ultimate chill-out zone? You can add toys, gadgets, furniture, books, pets, patterns and colours – whatever feels relaxing and comfy to you.

# ACTIVITY: RESILIENCE RUCKSACK

A resilience rucksack is a place to keep all the things that help you to feel strong and calm. You can use a box, shelf, bag or drawer – it doesn't need to be a rucksack if you don't have one spare.

What can go in a resilience rucksack?

Photos of family

Photos of friends

Photos of your favourite characters or celebrities

Photos of a pet

Soft teddies

Comfy hoodie or sweatshirt

This book!

Pens, pencils and paper

Bottle of water

Favourite books

Fidget toys

Cosy blanket

What will you put in your resilience rucksack? You can choose things from the list and think up your own, too – it's totally up to you. Write or draw your items below:

Having these things all in one place will help you to feel OK when you're dealing with change. When you feel nervous, worried or unsure, you can find your resilience rucksack and choose something to help you.

# ACTIVITY: DESIGN A MANDALA

Mandalas are round, symmetrical patterns which can help you feel calm, whether you're drawing one or colouring it in!

Here's a mandala – you can colour it in.

Now it's your turn to design your own mandala! Use the template to add your ideas – you can pick whichever shapes and patterns you like. Can you make yours symmetrical?

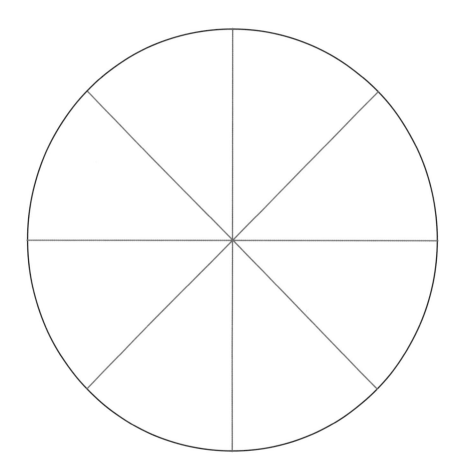

- **Symmetrical: the same on both sides, like a mirror reflection.**

I FEEL
CALM

# PART 7:
# A BRIGHT FUTURE

There's so much to look forward to! With the self-confidence that a resilient mindset gives you, you'll be able to feel strong, calm and positive through the changes that life brings you. In this chapter we'll celebrate the bright, resilient future ahead of you.

# ACTIVITY: SPREADING RESILIENCE

Now that you've learned so much about coping with change and building resilience, why not make a poster to help other children be kind to themselves during challenging times?

First, think about what your poster will say, or what the picture will show. Perhaps it could be something you learned in this book and didn't realize before, or some words that help you when you're dealing with change.

You can draw or paint, or use photos, pictures from a magazine, collage or cool lettering.

Sketch some ideas here:

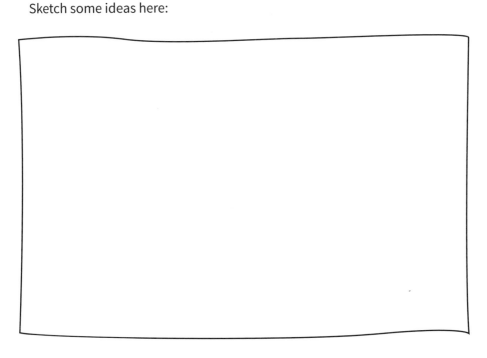

There's space on the next page for designing your poster neatly – remember: it's OK if your poster isn't perfect! Do your best and you'll inspire others.

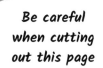

Be careful
when cutting
out this page

# ACTIVITY: WHAT ARE YOU LOOKING FORWARD TO?

Having something you're looking forward to builds motivation and helps you to stay positive, even when things are challenging.

Big events – like a holiday or a visit from your favourite cousins – are brilliant and it's so exciting to count down the days until they happen. But having something small to look forward to every day has a big effect on resilience.

Zig looks forward to a hot chocolate after school each day!

Perhaps there's already a part of your day that's your favourite – you can start looking forward to it, and thinking of it when your feet get cold, or a trip gets cancelled, or you get your least-favourite sandwich for lunch.

Here are some ideas:

*Watching an episode of my favourite show*

*Cuddling my pet*

*Climbing a tree on the way home*

*Waving to the bus driver*

*Going fast on my scooter*

*Singing along with the radio in the car*

What do you look forward to?

_____

_____

_____

_____

_____

_____

_____

# STORIES OF RESILIENCE

Dealing with change is tough, but amazing kids just like you show bravery and resilience every day. Here are just a few of their stories:

*My parents split up when I was eight, and that was a big change. It felt strange for a long time — getting used to having two houses, a new routine, and I felt very sad about it, too. I still feel sad sometimes, but the longer you do a new routine, the more comfortable it feels — it's normal now.*

Nisha, 10

*My birthday party got cancelled and I was so upset. I felt like my birthday was ruined. My mum sat with me while I cried, and let out my angry and disappointed feelings. I felt a bit better in the evening, and we went for a special meal at my favourite restaurant instead, so the day wasn't completely ruined.*

Milo, 7

*I was the first girl in my class to start my period, and it felt really scary that my body was changing. It took a lot of bravery to talk to my teacher, and I'm proud of myself for doing it. She was really understanding, showed me what to do and helped me feel OK.*

Grace, 11

*School was closed and we had to do our schoolwork at home. It was really hard — my parents both work so they were really busy and we all got stressed out. We made a promise to be as kind to each other and ourselves as we could, and we stuck to it. I'm glad to be back at school now!*

Jamie, 9

I AM
EXCITED AND
CURIOUS ABOUT
WHAT TODAY
WILL BRING

# MY RESILIENCE PLAN

In this book we've thought a lot about how to build resilience, and feel OK when change happens and we're going through a challenge. There have been lots of ideas – which ones work best for you? Let's make an action plan to help you feel calm, strong and resilient.

When I feel…

_____

I can talk to…

_____

I can write, say or think positive words like…

_____

I can calm my body by doing…

_____

I can say to others…

_____

# YOU CAN DO AMAZING THINGS
## GOLDEN RULES

Your feelings matter

You can take a break

It's OK to be yourself

Changes are difficult
and it's OK to ask
for help

You can do hard
and amazing things

# THE END

Zig's learned all about coping with change and building resilience – have you? You can come back to this book any time you like – whether you need a boost during a tough time, to help a friend understand resilience, or just to refresh your memory. You've worked really hard and should be very proud of yourself. Don't forget: when you're kind to yourself, you can do amazing things!

# I CAN DO AMAZING THINGS!

# For parents and carers: How to help build your child's resilience

Resilience is learned, so there are lots of ways you can help to build your child's strength in the face of challenges. This requires striking a balance between comforting them when they're feeling big emotions and trusting them to come up with their own solutions.

You know your child better than anyone, and you can trust yourself to get that balance right. Even if you make mistakes, you can learn from them and choose differently next time. In fact, one of the greatest gifts you can give your child is to model a positive, kind approach to making mistakes.

Research shows that spending one-on-one time with your child is a powerful way to grow their resilience and improve mental health. This is because children's emotional well-being comes from feeling secure in their relationships with the important people in their lives. Just five minutes of engaging with your child without distractions has a surprising effect on their ability to cope with change and adversity.

Another important component of resilience is self-care. Help your child to listen to what their body needs, and guide them toward healthy habits around sleep, eating and drinking. The better rested and nourished they are, the more able to cope with difficult emotions they'll be.

The world is changing at a dizzying rate, and it's a challenge for any of us to keep calm some days. Remember that it's healthy for your child to experience and express any kind of emotion – it doesn't mean they aren't resilient. On the contrary, being in touch with emotions and feeling comfortable expressing them is a sign of a resilient child and a secure, loving parent–child relationship.

I hope this book has been helpful. It's always hard to see your child dealing with difficult changes, and the instinct is often to protect them from challenging situations. Know that you are doing a fantastic job by supporting their emotional health.

# Further advice

If you're worried about your child's mental health, or you think they need extra support in the face of challenging situations, do talk it through with your doctor. While almost all children will struggle with certain changes, some may need extra help. There are lots of great resources out there for information and guidance on children's mental health:

**YoungMinds Parents' Helpline (UK)**
www.youngminds.org.uk
0808 802 5544

**BBC Bitesize (UK)**
www.bbc.co.uk/bitesize/support

**Childline (UK)**
www.childline.org.uk
0800 1111

**Child Mind Institute (USA)**
www.childmind.org

**The Youth Mental Health Project (USA)**
www.ymhproject.org

**UK Council for Psychotherapy**
www.psychotherapy.org.uk

**British Association for Counselling and Psychotherapy**
www.bacp.co.uk

# Recommended reading

....................................................................

*Letting Go! An Activity Book for Young People Who Need Support Through Experiences of Loss, Change, Disappointment and Grief* by Dr Sharie Coombes
Studio Press, 2020

*The Story Cure: An A–Z of Books to Keep Kids Happy, Healthy and Wise* by Ella Berthoud and Susan Elderkin
Canongate Books, 2017

*Happy, Healthy Minds: A Children's Guide to Emotional Wellbeing* by The School of Life and Lizzy Stewart
The School of Life Press, 2020

*My Feelings and Me: A Child's Guide to Understanding Emotions* by Poppy O'Neill
Vie, 2022

# Credits

pp.3, 13, 14, 28, 35, 40, 44, 51, 58, 60, 64, 66, 71, 75, 80, 87, 91, 98, 100, 114, 127, 130, 131, 137 – monsters © mers1na/Shutterstock.com; p.14 – journal and pen © RaulAlmu/Shutterstock.com; pp.24, 25, 92, 102 – shapes © wilkastok/Shutterstock.com; p.28 – cloud © Zahroe/Shutterstock.com; p.28 – superhero cape © Rashad Ashur/Shutterstock.com; p.29 – hand © Oleksandr Panasovskyi/Shutterstock.com; p.32 – child cuddling a pet © mijatmijatovic/Shutterstock.com; p.32 – child singing © mijatmijatovic/Shutterstock.com; p.33 – butterflies © Ekaterina kkch/Shutterstock.com; p.34 – colouring in page © SomjaiJaithieng/Shutterstock.com; p.35 – sandwich © QuoteMaker/Shutterstock.com; pp.35, 38, 39, 41, 44, 46, 58, 60, 61, 64, 71, 87, 107, 130, 132 – bubbles © Paket/Shutterstock.com; p.40 – bed © Ksenya Savva/Shutterstock.com; p.42 – painted pebbles © IrinaKrivoruchko/Shutterstock.com; pp.44, 64 – emoticons © SpicyTruffel/Shutterstock.com; p.46 – plant © My Flat Style/Shutterstock.com; p.46 – rain cloud © Zahroe/Shutterstock.com; p.47 – house plant © Briana Shore/Shutterstock.com; p.51 – watering can © Adila Jabbar/Shutterstock.com; p.51 – tree © Masilus Studio/Shutterstock.com; p.53 – child disappointed © mijatmijatovic/Shutterstock.com; p.63 – body outline © Anna Rassadnikova/Shutterstock.com; p.66 – ball © kosmofish/Shutterstock.com; p.69 – body parts © mijatmijatovic/Shutterstock.com; pp.75, 80 – suitcase © Vasilina/Shutterstock.com; p.76 – child in bed © mijatmijatovic/Shutterstock.com; p.77 – child playing a game © mijatmijatovic/Shutterstock.com; p.77 – child going to school © mijatmijatovic/Shutterstock.com; p.80 – house © Oliver Hoffmann/Shutterstock.com; p.88 – car © NEiDD/Shutterstock.com; p.88 – passport © GANJIRO KUMA/Shutterstock.com; p.88 – headphones © Anastasiia Novikova/Shutterstock.com; p.88 – plane landing © VoodooDot/Shutterstock.com; p.91 – maze © Vii Artist/Shutterstock.com; p.91 – rainbow © johavel/Shutterstock.com; p.98 – apple © Iryna Shyshkova/Shutterstock.com; p.103 – food items © Artco/Shutterstock.com; pp.110, 111 – yoga poses © Kudryashka/Shutterstock.com; p.114 – deck chair at the beach © Studio_G/Shutterstock.com; pp.120, 121 – bedroom © Aluna1/Shutterstock.com; p.123 – rucksack © Vectorfair/Shutterstock.com; p.124 – mandala © Semiankova Inha/Shutterstock.com; p.131 – hot chocolate © Sabuhi Novruzov/Shutterstock.com; p.136 – scroll © MasterGraph/Shutterstock.com

# THE WORRY WORKBOOK

The Worry Warriors' Activity Book

Imogen Harrison

£10.99

Paperback

ISBN: 978-1-78783-537-5

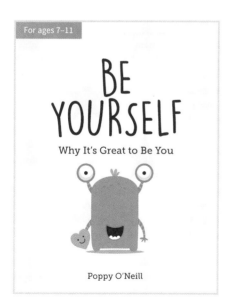

# BE YOURSELF

Why It's Great to Be You

Poppy O'Neill

£10.99

Paperback

ISBN: 978-1-78783-608-2

Have you enjoyed this book?
If so, why not write a review on your favourite website?

If you're interested in finding out more about our books,
find us on Facebook at **Summersdale Publishers,** on Twitter
at **@Summersdale** and on Instagram at **@summersdalebooks**
and get in touch. We'd love to hear from you!

Thanks very much for buying this Summersdale book.

**www.summersdale.com**